REFLECTIONS OF AN ORDINARY MAN

THOMAS S. BOZZUTO

©2018 Thomas S. Bozzuto
Sheridan Group, Inc.
3rd edition

Library of Congress Control Number: 201843589

ISBN: 978-0-692-16877-6

Edited by Adrienne Hand
Illustrated by Sarah Smith
Design Team: Chintimini Keith,
Samantha Schlemm, and Rebecca Breslin

Dedicated with love and admiration
to the most extraordinary person I know,
Barbara Bozzuto.

"Only he who keeps his eye fixed on the far horizon will find his right road."

Dag Hammarskjöld, Markings

Table of Contents

Foreword

As a U.S. Senator, one of my favorite parts of the job was holding roundtables with the public. My best ideas came from the people, and roundtables were my opportunity to listen to people who had problems and people who had solutions to those problems. Tom Bozzuto was one of those people always ready with solutions for many of the problems that Marylanders and Americans faced every day. Working closely with him throughout my time in the Senate, we worked to make homes more accessible and affordable by allowing business to build without cutting corners. By focusing on advocacy not bureaucracy and being the voice of the people we serve, we were able to make real change. And by the way, that is truly the way that Tom operates his business—his customers are the people he serves.

Tom has always brought passion, purpose, and performance to everything he does; here he gives us perspective, too. So many leaders all too often use the wrong "I" words: "I did this," or "I am taking credit for that." Not Tom. The "I" words that come to mind when I think of Tom Bozzuto are Intelligence, Insight, Inclusive, and, above all, Integrity.

This book reflects all that Tom is: his passion, his value-driven leadership, and his focus on living a life full of meaning and purpose. I am sure that as you read it, you will find that the guidelines Tom has shared for success in business and in life are not for speed reading. The commentary in these pages is more like sipping a glass of iced tea that refreshes, or pouring a glass of wine meant to savor a long day. It is the cup of coffee you drink as you search out how to organize your thinking for a project or solving a problem. Sit back and read a chapter a day, or all in one sitting. You will go back again and again to the wise words and practical counsel found here.

Barbara A. Mikulski

December 2017

Introduction

During the course of one's life, if your eyes, ears, and heart are open, you learn a few things. The following are some of the more important lessons I've learned. I truly hope they will be helpful and useful to anyone who reads them.

These are thoughts and reflections about life, love, and work accumulated over a long period of time. Whether in college, the army, my marriage, or during my career, I have spent time in thought and sought guidance. Books, especially biographies, have taught me a lot, and I've been blessed to talk with and learn from many smart people. I have tried to understand the rules governing a successful life and I've tried to live by them.

It has always seemed to me that the first rule is to know the rules.

In whatever manner one chooses to live one's life, it is important to be conscious of the rules of the game. Please understand that I am not suggesting life is a game that shouldn't be treated seriously. Rather, in everything we do—everything—there are rules, expectations, and guidelines that we need to understand and reflect on if we are to be successful.

So, where does one find guidelines to live by? Some, we learn from our parents and our family. Some from our church. Some, perhaps most, are discovered through trial and error as we go through life and learn lessons from experience. Others, and clearly many of those written here, are based on insights one can derive from books.

What I have found is that by discovering, noting, and reflecting on these guidelines, I have lived my life with what I believe has been a deeper sense of purpose and meaning than might otherwise have been the case.

Very early in my business career, when I first started writing down these reflections and some of what I've been told to describe as "prose poetry," they were merely notes in a journal—more for myself than for anyone else. However, as my kids grew, I decided to share my writing with each of them; so I did, by giving them a copy of most of what I had written as each was heading off to college.

Over time, especially as I've gotten older and have spent time in coaching and advisory roles, others seem to benefit from these reflections, as well. So, for whatever it's worth, I have decided to publish them, along with some of my prose poems.

Initially, I considered these guidelines to be rules for myself, rules to guide my life. Now that I am publishing them, I've tried to think of other ways to describe them. You can think of them as guidelines or reflections, or insights. Whatever works for you! For the purposes of this book, I am calling them "reflections" and numbering them. Further, where appropriate, I have elaborated on the thinking behind the reflection, although, as you will see, some simply stand on their own.

Much of what you will read in here is not original material. Where possible, I have given attribution to the person or source of the idea. If you should find something in here that you think was your idea first, please be my guest and take credit.

INTRODUCTION

The title, *Reflections of an Ordinary Man*, also needs explanation. I have always thought of myself as "ordinary," in the sense of not having special endowments or gifts. On the other hand, with very few exceptions, we are all ordinary; we are all equal, but we are able to distinguish ourselves with hard work, a willingness to think and to take risks, and a healthy dose of luck.

Use this book as you wish. You might want to read and mull over one reflection at a time. Or, you could turn to the Table of Contents to refer to a particular idea or issue that interests you at the moment. I just hope that these ponderings can be of some use to you. They have been reliable guideposts for me.

Finally, I must acknowledge that while I have written many of these reflections, and have been conscious of them all for many years, I have not always been able to live up to them. In fact, I've probably failed more than I've succeeded. I'm not proud of this, but I'm not ashamed to admit it either. I've tried!

Tom Bozzuto

April 2018

Part One

BUILDING A LIFE

DIGNITY AND INTEGRITY

Reflection

1

Your reputation is the loudest sound in the very small room that is your universe.

Reflection

2

**Never, ever value your enterprise, your business,
your success more than your personal integrity!**

Throughout my career, I have found that the line between "right" and "wrong" is seldom clear. It is not simply black or white; most of the time there is a substantial amount of gray between right and wrong. Nonetheless, there is a difference, and if you look hard enough, you will find that line. (It is, in fact, your responsibility to help others find the right thing to do, without being sanctimonious about it.)

It is thus very important that one be aware of this grayness, this ambiguity—and not allow oneself to be drawn into doing the wrong thing, inch by inch. The first inch, that first step, makes the next all too easy.

I have frequently reflected on the motivation of people who do immoral or illegal things. I believe that most are not inherently bad people. They are merely not focused on how easily actions in the gray area can, over time, allow them to slip into doing the wrong thing. So, remember to let your integrity guide your decision-making.

Reflection

3

Concern for others is the greatest virtue.

Read Jesus' Sermon on the Mount if you don't believe me. In this, his most important lesson, Jesus tells his disciples how to live a life that is dedicated to and pleasing to God, free from pretense, full of love and grace, and full of wisdom and good judgment. He taught that each of us can do this by loving one another.

How do we live a virtuous life today? We treat everyone with dignity. We treat everyone with concern. Smile and say hello to strangers. Try to remember their names. Listen when people talk—really listen. Don't just sit there thinking of your next response.

Concern for others is perhaps our greatest responsibility. "Concern" is The Bozzuto Group's most important value.

I learned to understand this idea by watching my father's relationship with his sisters. My dad was one of five children, falling somewhere in the middle in birth order. He was the only son. Every third or fourth Sunday, after church, my father would insist on taking my younger brother and me with him to visit his sisters. This wasn't like our frequent Saturday night get-togethers for family fun. This was a visit with each sister, in turn. We would go first to Aunt Josie's, because she was the oldest, and we would end the morning at Aunt Laurina's, because she was the "baby." At each home we'd be fed—sometimes homemade anisette cookies, sometimes pasta

8

fagiola (but never enough to ruin our appetites for my mother's dinner)—but we'd always eat a little something.

My father explained that, as the only man in the family, it was incumbent upon him to visit each sister, to make sure they were okay, but mostly to show his respect and his concern. Why this didn't happen on Saturday night when we had all the family around took me a while to understand. But ultimately, I came to realize that this "ritualized show of respect" was an important way for family and friends to treat each other.

I have tried to bring this idea into my business. At least one day a week for the past thirty-five years, I have gone out to visit properties we are building and managing. I visit the people on-site, people who are doing the work of our company and demonstrating the brand behavior for which the company is known. This is my way of showing them respect. It is also my way of showing them that I am concerned about them as individuals, that they are important to me and the company, not just for what they do, but for who they are.

Let's show thoughtfulness to others. Let's show compassion. Let's show we care. Think about how great the world would be if we all lived this way.

Reflection

4

"Dignity" is a virtue.
Never lose your dignity.

In the Western world, we are taught that the seven virtues are prudence, justice, temperance, courage, faith, hope, and charity. But to these I would add another, and that is "dignity". The dictionary defines dignity as the "state or quality of being worthy of honor or respect." I believe dignity is a sense of pride in oneself.

Try to carry yourself with a sense of purpose, pride, poise, and value, just as you would if you were handling the greatest gift God gave you.

Just as it is in your private life, dignity is essential also in business. Even in the most practical sense, I tell young people, "Every moment could be the one before a job interview." You never know who you will see next or, more importantly, who will see you. So carry yourself in such a way that you are able to take advantage of any opportunity.

A case in point. A few years back, while shopping at a CVS, I was so impressed by how well a fellow treated me—saying hello when I walked in, smiling, asking if I had found everything I was looking for—that I gave him my business card and told him to call if ever he wanted to change employment. Four weeks later he called, and he has been working for The Bozzuto Group now for three years.

10

DIGNITY AND INTEGRITY

While I believe that being treated with dignity and respect is something to which most people aspire, I am amazed by how little respect people sometimes show themselves. It's hard to imagine, then, how people who carry themselves poorly can expect you to respect them or treat them honorably. If you don't carry yourself in a way that commands respect, it is unlikely that you'll get it.

Reflection

5

**If you think you have reached your destination,
then you have given up the journey.**

Another variant of this rule is that if you have lived up to your
expectations of yourself, you have set the bar too low. Just because
you have accomplished something, you're not done. Life is about
the striving, not the arriving.

THE DECAMERON

As a man struggles to retain his youth,
he kicks against the
quickly closing envelope with
every tool at his command.

The tools can be terrible
or terrifying.
They can be real,
or
they can be myths.

Their purpose—to act like a straw
letting in a breath.

TSB
11/26/1992

Reflection

6

Your self-image is key to your success.

A person usually builds his own prison cell, sometimes by his actions, but more often by his self-conception. You are what you envision yourself to be. You can reach your full potential if and only if you enlarge your sense of what is possible and commit to that vision.

We are who we think we are. We can do what we think we can do. We hold ourselves back from achieving our optimal potential by our self-doubts. The words, "I could never do that..." almost guarantee that you won't.

This is not an argument for self-delusion or false conceit. Instead, it is an assertion that a man or woman can be only as successful or as accomplished as they imagine or project themselves to be—and then only if they commit to work to fulfill that vision. There is no successful concert pianist who, before going on stage, visualizes herself a failure.

If, instead, we visualize ourselves as successful in everything we are about to do, and combine that with a great deal of practice, we will surprise ourselves with what we can achieve.

I have found that even visualizing an achievement unrelated to the task at hand, such as a batter with a beautiful swing hitting a baseball out of the park, helps me prepare to undertake a task that might otherwise be intimidating.

DIGNITY AND INTEGRITY

So do not define yourself by your limitations, your handicaps, the least about yourself. Define yourself, instead, by the best about who you are, and you will have a much greater chance of success.

Reflection

7

Everything is possible!

Some social scientists say that economic mobility is harder in America today than it was in the past. Others say the contrary. I strongly believe it is still possible. Look at the most successful people in our society and you will find that the vast majority were not born rich. They worked endlessly. They took chances fearlessly and they proceeded step by step. Everything is still possible!

In the early part of the twentieth century, every schoolchild read Horatio Alger stories—profiles of people who were notable for their perseverance, integrity, and commitment to excellence in the face of great adversity. Today, these stories are not as prevalent. And yet if one were to look at almost any list of very successful people, you would see that a great many of them started with very little.

Former New York City Mayor Michael Bloomberg's parents were Eastern European immigrants. His father was a bookkeeper. Sam Walton, the founder of Walmart, was the son of a farmer who had to become a mortgage broker because he couldn't support his family.

Supreme Court Justice Ruth Bader Ginsburg was born to Russian Jewish immigrants and was a wife and mother before starting law school. Ursula Burns, the former chairwoman and CEO of Xerox, was raised by a single mother in a New York City public housing project. Larry Ellison, the founder of Oracle, was born to an unwed mother who, after contracting pneumonia, gave him up to her aunt and uncle for adoption when he was nine months old.

Certainly, luck has also played a great role in the success of these men and women. And I know for certain that my wife and I have been very fortunate. We were blessed with good parents, albeit of modest means. We were both lucky to be encouraged and supported, and we were able to attend good colleges. But when we finished school and moved to Baltimore, we had $370 in our bank account. (Being newlyweds, we spent $300 of that on a mattress.) In addition, we had $10,000 in student debt. We worked hard and earned a living. We took risks. We were willing to take steps backwards, financially, if we thought it would help us get ahead.

With my wife's consistent support, I changed jobs five times in my career, including when I formed a partnership and started The Bozzuto Group. Each time, I took a reduction in pay (once or twice, significantly), betting that a new position would offer a superior long-term opportunity. Not all of these bets paid off. In one case, I started a company with another fellow and within two years, I realized that we were so incompatible that it would just never work out. So, we agreed to an amiable dissolution of the company, and I moved on.

Perhaps I got lucky with each of the other career moves, but certainly, my willingness to take risks and bet on myself, and my wife's willingness to support me—not only with words but also with hard work—made it possible for us to achieve a fair amount of personal and professional success.

So yes, I believe America is still a land of great opportunity. One just has to be willing to work hard. And, of course, have a little luck.

Reflection

8

"Choice, not chance, determines destiny."

Aristotle, as quoted by Dr. Freeman Hrabowski III,
President of the University of Maryland, Baltimore County

We are who we are to a very significant degree because of the choices and decisions we make. We all have some limitations as a result of our circumstances—our parents, our environment, our economic status—but we are also given opportunities, and what we make of our lives is very much in our hands. Our destiny completely depends on the decisions we make on a daily basis.

In the novel *The Lay of the Land*, by Richard Ford, one character says, "The things you'll never do don't get decided at the end of life, but somewhere in the long gray middle...."

As we go through our lives, we make countless decisions, and perhaps avoid many others. It is by these decisions that we are making the choices that will determine our fate. We must make them wisely.

PASSION

Reflection
9

"It is not the critic who counts... The credit belongs to the man who is actually in the arena, whose face is marred by dust and sweat and blood; who strives valiantly; who errs, who comes short again and again... who knows the great enthusiasms, the great devotions; who spends himself in a worthy cause; who at the best knows in the end the triumph of high achievement, and who at the worst, if he fails, at least fails while daring greatly, so that his place shall never be with those cold and timid souls who neither know victory nor defeat."

Theodore Roosevelt, 26th President of the United States

I framed this statement and kept it on my bedroom wall throughout my teenage years. Not all of us are destined to be president, nor to be great leaders, nor people who change the world. But the person who leads a full life is one who strives to leave the world a better place than he or she found it; one who pushes oneself to take risks; one who tries to accomplish something that leaves a lasting legacy.

Reflection
10

Give 'em hell, always!

When my children were young and about to play a game, take a test, or ride a horse in a competition, I used to say to them: "Give 'em hell!"

Over the years, I've recognized that the expression, "Give 'em hell!" contains a nugget of truth as important as any in this collection. A colloquialism that evolved long ago out of 33rd President of the United States Harry Truman's presidential campaign, it was meant then, and I have meant since, that you must bring extraordinary commitment and passion to everything you do. You must be "all in" with everything you do. And you must bring your concentration, your energy, your joy, and especially your passion to whatever it is you want to achieve.

Give 'em hell!

Reflection

11

"... live in the game and die in it."

Stubbs, in the novel Moby Dick, *by Herman Melville*

Most of us have the opportunity to live fully until we die—so why do some of us fail to do so? There are people who can't wait to stop working—not so they can spend their time pursuing a goal that is important to them. Instead, they can't wait to retire so they can relax and do absolutely nothing. I really don't understand this.

It seems to me that we should be aware of how valuable our short time on this earth is. We should want to make the most of it. Each of us can define our own goals, but let's always have goals—this is what it means to be alive. Spend some time thinking about what is most important to you. Even if you are not concerned about leaving a legacy, you should be concerned about leading a full and meaningful life.

To the degree that one's health will allow, one should live one's life so that their death is a surprise.

I wrote all of the above when I was much younger than I am today. I was years away from what we think of as retirement age. But as I reflect on it today, and as I get closer to an age where death won't be a complete surprise, I feel even more strongly than I did years ago that one should treasure each moment, make it count, and try to live a life that matters—a life of consequence.

FISHING WITH WHALES

In awe of nature,
but part of nature
and thus, not afraid.

Twenty-five miles offshore,
no land to be seen,
no other boats,
only birds, gulls, ducks,
and terns.
And, oh yes,
whales.

All around me, and below me.
(I saw their bubbles.)

Alone, away from (other) man
but not away from sound,
the noise
of the birds,
the waves licking my boat,
the bassoon of the whales
—all around me.
A very pretty concert.

Alone, except
an occasional dot on the horizon,
several commercial trawlers,
a sport fisher or two.

Alone, except
a small plane flying over
too low
waving its wings
in silent salutation.

PASSION

Alone, except
a chart telling
where I was
and a compass telling me
how I got here and
how to get back.

Alone, except,
finally, a tug on the
end of my line—
a shark
to be thrown back
into the awesome Atlantic
followed within minutes
by codfish—one, two, three cod
plenty more there for the taking,
but why be greedy?

Besides, I had promised Barb
I'd be in by nine and
it was already five past.

Alone, except
for my boat.

Alone, and yet
my oneness with my surroundings—
the sea, the sky, the sun—
whales, fish, birds, and
my craft

renders the word "alone"
meaningless.

TSB
7/26/1978, Chatham

31

Reflection

12

Push yourself out of your comfort zone at least once every single day. Go where your fear is!

So many of us hesitate to do things that make us uncomfortable, whether it's to offer an idea in a classroom, to disagree with the prevailing opinion, or to raise our hand for a new job opportunity. We are afraid of failure. But, so what if you fail? We learn from our failures. We grow from our failures. And most of us know that.

I believe what we are really afraid of is the crawling, queasy, almost nauseous feeling in our gut that comes when we take a risk. Learn to love that feeling, and you will be surprised at just how successful you might be. Make that feeling your friend. Welcome it and understand that it is only your adrenaline preparing you for the next challenge.

I know a fellow whose boss came to him one day and said, "You're so good at what you do, I want you to start teaching classes to your colleagues around the country, on how to do it." This terrified the fellow because he had always been exceptionally shy and generally tried to make himself invisible in social situations. He was a very hard worker, though, and he prepped for this challenge like he did anything else: carefully, thoughtfully, and with great effort. In the end, not only did he succeed, but in the process of facing his fears, he honestly changed his entire personality.

Yet another example: I had an aunt who never left the confines of the city in Connecticut where she was born. I'm not exaggerating. When, finally, my father took her on a tour of the Mid-Atlantic states, she was in awe of what she had missed. She was in her seventies.

There are so many people who let fear of being uncomfortable limit their potential. Perhaps not quite as much as my aunt, but they do stifle their growth by avoiding risks. As a result, they fail to achieve their full potential. Perhaps more importantly, they fail to enjoy the beauty that life offers.

Reflection
13

"For, as I like a young man in whom there is something of the old, so I like an old man in whom there is something of the young; and he who follows this maxim, in body will possibly be an old man, but he will never be an old man in mind."

Cicero, Roman politician and lawyer, 106 BC–43 BC

For anyone who has had the occasion to go to his or her fiftieth high school reunion, or maybe even a fortieth, the truth of Cicero's statement will be obvious. Looking around the room, you see some people who have the vitality and dynamism they had when they were in school, and then you see others who have decided they are old. These are the ones who appear tired and perhaps defeated. They look as though the only thing they have to look forward to is their own funeral.

Don't be a fool, but always be grateful if the number of candles on your birthday cake exceeds the years you feel. Or, as baseball legend Satchel Paige once asked: "How old would you be if you didn't know how old you are?"

Reflection

14

In many ways, fishing is like living.
They are both better done on your feet.

I am a passionate fly fisherman. I love being outdoors, enjoying nature's beauty. (I always say, "Trout don't live in ugly places.") I take joy in the challenge of matching the hatch, the art of casting, and especially the intimacy of the contact between the living, fighting fish and my hands uniquely felt through a fly rod.

So you can understand my surprise when a neighbor asked me one day what I daydreamed about while I fished. I guess she had a Norman Rockwellesque view of me sitting on the end of a dock with my feet dangling into the water, a pipe in my mouth and a rod in my hand.

No, I fish the way I believe one should live—with passion, focus, and energy. I fish with concentration on the river current, on the fly, and on the fish. I fish on my feet. And that's how I try to live my life.

ROCKFISH RECIPE

Baking pan covered with olive oil.
Place fish in pan, skin down.
Cover fish with more olive oil
and smother with onion—completely.
Put on dill seed and Italian seasoning.
Bake till done.
Serve with lime
and eat with the daughter you adore.

TSB
6/1996

Reflection

15

"Imagination is more important than knowledge. For knowledge is limited to all we now know and understand, while imagination embraces the entire world, and all there ever will be to know and understand."

Albert Einstein, theoretical physicist

Einstein attributed his greatness not to his intelligence, but to his willingness to ask questions and search creatively for answers. In fact, as a child, Einstein was a poor student. But because of his creativity, his willingness to ask big questions, he became one of the most influential thinkers of the twentieth century.

Few of us have Einstein's intellect, but each of us has the opportunity to push ourselves beyond what we see.

Reflection
16

"Today is a good day to die!"
What a wonderful guide for living.
Live life as if it is about to end.

Quotation attributed to Crazy Horse, Lakota war
leader, before the Battle of the Little Bighorn

We've all read stories about people who changed their lives when
they learned that death was imminent. I've always wondered why
one would wait for such an event before figuring out how one wants
to live, or what is important.

We all know we are going to die. We just don't know when. We
can be fortunate and die at a ripe old age—or not. It seems silly to
me to think that God owes us an advance warning so that we have
time to prepare. Live your life like it will end today. Leave nothing
to regret; live to the fullest. Always be able to say, "I have done
everything I could. I have lived every moment God has given me."

Just as you live your own life with an awareness of your mortality,
you should also make sure your children grow into adults who do
the same. Teach them that life is precious and short. Teach them
that every moment counts. Teach them that they too will die.

Reflection
17

Be passionate!
Reserve is for the funeral home.

Strive to do as much, live as much, accomplish as much, sample life as much as you possibly can. Life is finite. You can rest when you're in the grave.

EVERYDAY LIFE

NEW YEAR'S DAY

As I sit here on New Year's Day
with my beautiful son playing by my side
in the den of our first home,
and hear you moving pots and pans downstairs,
the sun shines in on my life
and I am happy.

TSB
1/1/1975

Reflection

18

"Find a way to make beauty necessary.
Find a way to make necessity beautiful."

Anne Michaels, in the novel Fugitive Pieces

I have long wondered why so much of what we do in life, we do automatically and without thought. If we live unaware of the beauty and variety around us, the result will be that there is nothing aesthetically satisfying in our daily lives. And that is not only unfortunate, it is unforgiveable.

There is so much beauty around us and there is so much that we can do to make our environment beautiful. It seems that our lives are only half-full when we don't take a moment to look around and enjoy that feast.

My wife Barbara and I have long collected art. Taking the advice that her artist uncle, Ed Giobbi, gave us early in our marriage, we collected what we loved, not caring whether the artist was well-regarded by others, and, where possible, we bought directly from the artist. We did not spend a lot of money on our art, but we do love every piece we own.

Nonetheless, while on a mission of one sort or another, I frequently zip from one end of the house to the other without looking. The artwork is there. Paintings and pieces of sculpture that my wife and I chose because they were meaningful and beautiful. I just know my life would be even better than it is if I would stop and truly appreciate what we have.

But that only addresses "making beauty necessary," making it an important part of every day. It doesn't speak to the other part of this reflection—"making necessity beautiful." This is important to me because it suggests that everything we do, including the everyday stuff we have to do, can be done with style. It can be made attractive. And, in making it so, there is a kind of pride beyond that which we get from merely completing a job.

For example, think about your home and surroundings. When you have put so much of yourself into making your home beautiful, take time to notice the things that make it so. And don't allow your home to be disfigured by clutter. Instead, take pride in your surroundings.

Consider the advice of the artist William Morris. His idea was that people should be surrounded by beautiful, useful things—a vision that sparked the Arts and Crafts movement in America. He said, "Have nothing in your house that you do not know to be useful, or believe to be beautiful."

I completely agree. For there is nothing worth doing that isn't worth doing in a beautiful manner. Add beauty to your life; look for it every day.

MY FAVORITE TIME

No, it's not standing
in a stream
or
on my boat
with my fly rod in hand,

though I do love that.

No, it's not being
at work
with my partners and colleagues,
even if you think
it is,

though I do love that.

No, it's not even when
I'm with my grandchildren,
whose very breathing
I find fascinating and like poetry,

though, God yes, I do love that.

No, my beautiful wife,
my favorite time
is when we sit at the dinner table,
just the two of us;
dinner finished,
me with my cigar,
each of us with a glass of wine.

Those blessed moments
of conversation,
of communication,
of communion.

54

EVERYDAY LIFE

Hours spent
reviewing the day,
sharing ideas,
talking about the past,
speculating about the future.

That, my love,
is my favorite time.

TSB
10/2017

Reflection

19

Remember every moment.
"If this isn't nice, what is?"

Kilgore Trout in the novel Timequake, *by Kurt Vonnegut*

Kilgore Trout, a hilarious fictional character created by Kurt Vonnegut, offers a treasure of great wisdom. In this quote, Trout reminds us that we should notice when we are happy. We frequently don't realize how much of what we do on a day-to-day basis is enjoyable. Maybe it's not over the top, scream from the rafters fun, but it's enjoyable—if only we would notice.

Indeed, we should ask ourselves as we go about our daily routine—whether it be walking the dog, having a meal, reading to our kids, enjoying the smell of brewing coffee, the sound of migrating geese, or the peace of sitting quietly at our desk working, "If this isn't nice, what is?"

Remember to enjoy these little things; they are the color that fills the heart and makes one's life joyful.

Reflection

20

Learn to say "no."

When you say "yes" but mean "no," don't make others suffer from your lack of discipline.

Many times we agree to things reluctantly and against our better judgment, and then act peevishly as we "go along." Unless we are truly indifferent to any outcome of our choice, we should make our position clear and stand by our decision. If you do agree to do something you'd prefer not to do, and of course more than half of life is about making such compromises—then get over it. Don't spend time regretting that you didn't have the backbone to say "no." Don't go along and then make everyone else miserable. Learn to say "no."

LOVE, FAMILY, AND FRIENDS

Reflection
21

Without love, there can be no life!

In most respects, this should be Reflection 1. Life without love will be hollow and fruitless.

A PRAYER ON A GRANDSON

My Lord in heaven,
cast your loving eyes
and gentle hand
on the child
who will be born tomorrow.

With your will, his birth
will be easy, his mother's burden light.

With your grace, his life
will be full, and fulfilling.

Help him to be a good man,
a kind man,
and
a man who knows your love.

And thank you, Lord.

TSB
3/18/2008

Reflection

22

Find a lover. Keep her always.

What elaboration or explanation can this possibly need? I found mine almost half a century ago and I am who I am for having done so.

HOME EQUALS SANCTUARY

My thought today,
as I approach my home,
our tree house,
after a long day,
a longer week:

Sanctuary... a place of total comfort,
security, and freedom.
Especially freedom from
false faces.

Home—Family—Warmth—Barbara.

My sanctuary.

TSB
5/1997

Reflection
23

A father and a mother, first and foremost, provide their family "sanctuary": a place of love, peace, safety, and tranquility.

A FATHER

A comforter who frightens away the bogeyman
from a child's sleep.

The outer-ring of the wheel
which is a family,
not as important as the
center-ring or hub, the mother,
in holding the family together,
but important just the same—
He's the one who provides direction.

TSB
6/15/1977

Reflection
24

A family is the blood that allows one's heart to beat.

If at all possible, have a family. Watching and helping children grow is not only fun and personally fulfilling, but it gives you a perspective and understanding of life and love that you cannot get anywhere else.

If you don't have children of your own, then find some to tutor, to coach, or to mentor. I think it is our responsibility to God to prepare the next generation.

No matter how busy your life, nor how important your job, find time to spend with your family. You will find that it is the best thing you can do for yourself. Time spent with family is as nourishing to the soul as blood is to your heart.

SIXTEEN

A child grows
and a father is proud,

the job is by far not done,
the responsibility still there.

But the results have begun to show
and the boy is good to know.

A son matures
and a parent remembers the effort.
There has often been conflict,
their egos clashing.

But the results have begun to show
and the boy is good to know.

A man appears
and a family applauds.
He is tall and handsome and smart.
He is sixteen.

Yes, the results have begun to show
and the boy is good to know.

TSB
4/16/1990

Reflection
25

Always talk with and listen to your spouse.

Through the years, I have received better advice from my wife Barbara than from anyone else. I have found that having her fully aware of what I am working on, thinking about, struggling with, has made us true partners. In fact, we are far more than partners. I have often thought of my wife as a great wine and myself as the glass in which to enjoy her. We are one. I know she would say the same about me.

FLYING EQUESTRIAN

Watching Lexie ride
with her head held high,
her back so straight
she rides her horse
like an eagle
in flight.

The prize for skill is a ribbon.
It should be a feather.

TSB
10/29/1990

Reflection
26

**Choose as friends those who think and love ideas.
Everyone else will turn your mind to mush.**

Did you ever notice the number of people who sit idly through conversations, avoiding any discussion of difficult or thought-provoking questions? Life can be so much more invigorating and enjoyable if you spend time with people who like ideas and are willing to discuss them. Yes, even politics and religion.

SPIRITUALITY AND
LIVING A VIRTUOUS LIFE

Reflection

27

Remember to begin each prayer with, "Thank you."

So much of prayer, dating back at least to Psalms, is about imploring the Lord for something. Even today, we compose most of our prayers to appeal to this great Big Poppa in the sky to whom we go when we want something we can't provide ourselves. What if instead, before we begin our prayers, we really look around at all of our blessings, at life itself, the beauty around us, the breath of air we just took? I believe we would then be embarrassed to start any discussion with God without first saying the words, "Thank you."

Reflection

28

"The most beautiful thing we can experience is the mysterious. It is the source of all true art and science."

Albert Einstein, theoretical physicist

It is what we don't know that motivates us to think, to learn, and to investigate. It is what we don't know and what intrigues us that make all of our intellectual growth possible.

My wife and I are both voracious readers, each of us working through thirty to forty books a year and, being who we are, even competing to see who can read the most. My books vary from novels and biographies to science, history, science fiction, and books about housing and cities. Barbara reads novels and biographies, especially of musicians. There is so much that is mysterious, so much to know—and we still know so little. It is important to us to always keep learning.

Reflection

29

Leave the Earth at least as beautiful as it was the day you were born.

This was a reflection often put forth by Ray Blank, who was for many years our corporate and my personal consultant. I used to call Ray our "Corporate Yoda" because, like the *Star Wars* character, he often had brilliant advice but made you work to discover it for yourself. Ray believed each of us had a responsibility to leave the earth as we found it.

Perhaps I'm more demanding than Ray, but I believe we all have a responsibility to try to make our Earth even more beautiful than we found it. Certainly, as a builder, I feel an increased responsibility to ensure that nothing The Bozzuto Group builds distracts from Earth's natural beauty, but rather improves upon it.

Reflection

30

"... so in the soul of man, there lies one insular Tahiti, full of peace and joy, but encompassed by all the horrors of the half-known life."

Ishmael, in the novel Moby Dick, *by Herman Melville*

There is so much we do every day, so much distraction. We need to stop and think about what it is that really makes our souls full, what makes us feel whole. This is our Tahiti.

Find that Tahiti in yourself. Find what gives you joy—not momentary pleasure—but true joy.

Reflection
31

"Alas! No rest the guilty find from the pursuing furies of the mind."

Dejanira, in the musical drama Hercules, *by George Frideric Handel*

Dejanira, the jealous wife and inadvertent murderess of Hercules, reminds us that no matter how well we fool the rest of the world, we cannot hide from our own failing and deceit.

Reflection

32

**Remember the "categorical imperative"
as defined by German philosopher Immanuel
Kant. You determine what is "okay" and necessary
for your fellow beings by your own actions.**

Kant wrote, "Act only according to that maxim whereby you can at the same time will that it should become a universal law."

As I understand this, what the philosopher is saying is that when you choose what to do, what is acceptable behavior for you, you are acknowledging that you believe everyone can or should be able to do the same.

If you treat people with respect, you are modeling that behavior for others to follow. If you steal or cheat, you are giving authority to everyone else to steal or cheat—even from you.

Learn this, and live by it. After the Ten Commandments and Jesus' Sermon on the Mount, this is the best guide I know for making decisions.

Reflection
33

**Knowledge is meaningless without wisdom,
and wisdom requires spirituality.**

We all know well-educated, highly intelligent people who don't have the wisdom to use that intelligence productively or constructively. To use one's intelligence wisely requires that one recognize the larger construct of his situation, the way one fits into the world, and what we can bring to any situation. I believe we cannot have that wisdom without understanding how we relate to others, how we relate to our environment, and how we relate to God.

This wisdom is not exclusively the province of the aged. We've all known older people who were the same damned fools they were when they were young. Wisdom comes to those who ask the big questions and try to understand where they fit and how they contribute to the larger world.

Reflection

34

According to St. Paul, John the Baptist said that to prepare for the arrival of the Lord, a rich man should share his wealth with the poor and a powerful man should not use power to take advantage of the weak.

This doesn't seem a lot to ask!

In fact, charity, sharing our blessings with others, is everyone's responsibility. Just as we should show concern and understanding for each other, we should share a portion of our wealth, no matter how meager, with those who have less. And by "wealth" I am not referring merely to money. The gift of volunteering time to help improve our community is as valuable as money.

The need is always so great that no matter how much money you give, or how much time, it will always feel inadequate. So remember, regardless of what or how much you have, you are blessed, and as such, have a responsibility to share those blessings with others.

RANDOM THOUGHTS
ON THE COLLAPSE OF
SOUTH VIETNAM

A one-year war for me
a ten-year war for America
a thirty-year war for the Vietnamese.

So many wasted years
so much wasted money
so many wasted lives.

For what?

Homes?
Food?

NO!

For Death!
For Capitalism!
For Communism!
For national unity!

For Christ's sake!

Why do people so consistently refuse to act intelligently?
Why do old men send young ones to die?

TSB
4/12/1975

Reflection

35

"No glory is it for an eagle to have overcome a dove."

The Decameron, *a collection of fourteenth-century stories by Giovanni Boccaccio*

Never take pride in easy success. So often, our success in business comes not as a result of our own virtue or prowess, but as a result of the weakness or mistakes of our competitors. False pride is probably the most self-destructive of the great vices.

Reflection
36

"Don't think you've hit a triple
when you were born on third base."

Borrowed from Coach Barry Switzer

"I drink deeply from the wells of freedom and liberty I did not dig. I eat lavishly from banquet tables prepared for me by ancestors. I sit under the shade of trees that were planted and cultivated and cared for by those I will never know..."

Cory Booker, then Mayor of Newark, New Jersey, spoke these words to the Bard College graduating class of 2009. There is little I can add to this that would improve upon it.

Be grateful every day!

Reflection
37

**There is no person more often wrong
than the one who always thinks he's right.**

Nothing is more tedious than self-righteousness.

The self-righteous sit in judgment on us all. They have no
compassion, no mercy, and usually, no sense of perspective. They
are predictable, painful to listen to, and usually, just plain boring.

Reflection

38

When you buy a dog, let it do its own barking.

I'm sure I didn't make this up, but I love it nonetheless. Perhaps it's because I love dogs, and most people I like have dogs, but it's probably because I love the idea here which is, quite simply: "Don't brag." Let your performance, your success, your achievements speak for themselves.

Reflection
39

Have fun—remember to laugh!

Laughter is the sound of God coming though us.

Life is very short. If you don't bring joy to what you're doing, you will seldom be successful or truly happy. And if you find that you can't bring joy to what you're doing, by all means, do something else.

Part Two

BUILDING A BUSINESS

LEADING PEOPLE

Reflection

40

The key to leadership is trust.
Without integrity, there can be no trust.

I have long pondered the keys to successful leadership. There are as many different types of leaders and leadership styles as there are enterprises. However, one of the things of which I am absolutely sure is that no one will follow you anywhere if they don't trust that you have their interest at heart. If they think you look at them as a pawn, they may follow for a while, but it will only be until their next opportunity. You need to care about the people on your team if you want them to stay on your team.

People also need to know that you honestly believe and will do what you say. This is leading with integrity, and it is how we build trust.

Reflection

41

A good leader selects the best people he can find, points the direction, makes clear the mission, establishes the value system by which they are expected to behave, encourages, cajoles, trains, and coaches, and then gets the hell out of their way.

Too often, people building organizations limit the growth of their enterprises because they are afraid to trust those they have hired. For an organization to grow and prosper, a leader must be willing to allow those working there to grow and prosper as well. It is one of life's great ironies that to be a successful leader, one must have a strong ego, yet must be willing to subordinate it enough to allow the egos of those with whom you work to shine through.

The leader must also be willing to allow people to make mistakes. People learn and grow only if allowed to do so. A corporate culture in which mistakes are punished is one that will soon fail.

Reflection

42

Leaders lead...
managers often just get in the way.

Warren G. Bennis, perhaps America's foremost expert in the field of leadership, once said: "Managers do things right. Leaders do the right thing."

It is important to distinguish "leadership" from "management." There are a lot of managers in the world, and there are people who "run departments" and organizations. While I know we need managers, there is a world of difference between being a manager and being a leader.

Let me be clear that I am not talking about titles here. At one point in our lives, many of us are called "managers." But there are managers who are great leaders, and then there are managers who are, well, just managers.

A leader sets the direction clearly for the people with whom she has formed a team. A leader makes sure the team knows her expectations, value system, and goals and then allows her people to do their job. A manager insists on close oversight, and is all too often ruled by fear of mistakes.

A leader is willing to take chances. A leader grooms her people. A manager fears challengers from within and without. A leader shows confidence in her people. A manager seldom does.

Regardless of your job title, be a leader.

Reflection
43

Talent doesn't discriminate.

When I was a young boy, I had a number of odd jobs, from shining shoes to delivering papers. In my thirteenth summer, I was a caddy at the country club in my hometown. After one entire day of caddying something like twenty-seven holes, having enjoyed the great sociability and beauty of the place, I came home and told my dad that when I grew up, I intended to join that club. He looked at me with more concern on his face than I usually saw there, and said, "Tommy, I wouldn't set your heart on that. You'll never get in. They don't allow Italians!"

While I know my first experience with bigotry pales when compared to what many people of color or women experience, it was enough to create a permanent impression that has led me throughout my life to resist the tendency to categorize or type people other than by their talent and their character.

What I have found in my business is that talent is pretty evenly spread across gender, race, religion, and national origin. When we at Bozzuto hire, we care more about how hard you're willing to work than where you're from, whether you're male or female, or your sexual preference. We care most about your ethics and how you treat people and whether you are a nice person.

I also know that if, as an executive, you exclude women from leadership roles, you're excluding half of the population. And you're a damn fool if you don't look for talent wherever you can find it. There are certainly as many brilliant women as there are brilliant men. I don't think you can generalize about women's and men's business skills or even their approaches to people or decision-making. When you're hiring, just remember that talent doesn't discriminate by gender or nationality. Neither does character.

Even though my hometown country club has changed its policy over the years and has welcomed members of my family, I am grateful for the early lesson in bigotry it provided me.

Reflection

44

There is a lesson to be learned from a rainbow.

I have long believed that we should surround ourselves with people whose talent and character we value, regardless of their gender, race, or creed. It was upon that belief that we built The Bozzuto Group. But it has only been in later years that I realized there was strength—real strength—that came to our company as a result of that rich diversity.

It seems to me that in just the same way that a rainbow outshines and dominates the rest of the sky, a group of diverse people who come together for a common purpose brings a greater variety of perspectives and approaches to problem-solving. Those of us from different backgrounds may bring different viewpoints and perspectives to the table—and that is all for the good. In my experience, such inclusiveness enhances and contributes to a greater level of creativity than you would likely find when a group is made up of people who all look alike and have similar backgrounds. And, creativity—the willingness and ability to adapt and change—is the single most important factor for an organization's long-term success.

The lesson of the rainbow is not that we should avoid hiring based solely on skin color, gender, or nationality. It is that groups and organizations tend to thrive and grow as a direct result of such diversity.

Reflection

45

It's always about the people. Always.

When success comes, give credit to the people who made it happen. They did make it happen. Conversely, failure is not an orphan. Someone is responsible. Help them get better, or move on.

I have often found that when I compliment or congratulate a leader who has done a particularly good job, he or she instinctively and immediately gives credit to their team. I believe this is a hallmark of real leadership, and has been throughout history. By example, when French Military Leader and Emperor Napoleon Bonaparte was first building his reputation as a military officer, he spent a great deal of his time writing up citations and commendations, and then later providing spoils of war to those among his troops who showed the greatest courage and gallantry.

Very few of us accomplish anything by ourselves. We succeed or fail with the help of others. Recognize it. And recognize them.

Reflection

46

A good leader always applauds.

This seems like such an unnecessary reflection until one has the unfortunate experience of working for someone who is unwilling or does not know how to pay a compliment. People work for praise! Yes, they also work for money and personal fulfillment, but few things consistently motivate people like recognition of work well accomplished.

I understand that there are many reasons people work. But beyond a certain level of compensation, praise for a job well done usually becomes most important.

Reflection

47

Anything "high performance"—a car, a boat, a racehorse, another person—will require lots of attention and special handling.

I've always loved high-end, fancy automobiles and I've owned BMWs, Jaguars, Lincolns, and Mercedes, as well as a few European sports cars. The one lesson I've taken away from owning these is that the fancier something is, and the more other people envy you for having it, the more time and money you will have to spend to keep it running.

When you think about business, the same can be said about those special people who are the stars of the team. As a leader, you need to make everyone feel important, but generally, you'll want to take special care of those who are high performers. Teach them, mentor them. For after all, they are often where you have made your highest investment and where you'll receive your greatest return. Your business culture will thrive with such attention and care.

TIME

As a bee lives to pollinate,
a man lives to create.

Just because a man ages,
he needn't stop being
a man.

But to be a man
and to be creative,
one must learn to control
time;
not let time control him.

TSB
1/2017

Reflection
_____
48

**People won't care what you know
until they know that you care.**

Derived from Theodore Roosevelt, 26ᵗʰ President of the United States

People need to know you care—care about them, care about what's important to them, care about their future, and truly care about what you're working on together—before they will even listen to you.

Reflection

49

**There is a difference between being "tough"
and being "mean." One should applaud
the former and avoid the latter.**

Being "tough-minded" is being able to analyze one's choices carefully and make a decision despite knowing that the consequences of that decision might be unpopular. This is critical to success in business. There will be times, for example, when someone has to be let go because he or she simply doesn't contribute to the success of the enterprise. Often, that person is a "nice person," has a family, and even works hard. The right decision, the decision to let him go, is frequently the most difficult choice any of us ever make in business. It is so important to handle that difficult conversation with consideration and care. But make the decision.

Unfortunately, during my business career I have met people who can't differentiate between being tough and being mean. They may think they are being tough when, in fact, they appear absolutely callous or at least indifferent to the fact that they are working with human beings.

There is no pride point in being a bully. Long-term success comes to those who can do the right thing and be compassionate while doing so.

Reflection

50

The best leader is one who listens to those he is to serve.

As a leader, we have the responsibility to keep the entire organization focused on the needs of our customers. The organization can best do that by listening carefully to its customers. The leader can ensure that this happens by first encouraging his colleagues to do so, and then, in turn, by listening to those who have direct contact with the customers. A culture that encourages careful listening and understanding will have a greater chance of success than any other.

Reflection

51

An organization, to be successful, should have only two kinds of people—great and gone!

This is one of those rules that none of us can live by all of the time, but it is one we should never forget. Otherwise, it is too easy to accept mediocrity. Every time we evaluate those we work with, we should ask ourselves if they are the best people available to do the job, or if, with time and training, they could be.

If not, we should ask ourselves why they are there.

Reflection

52

Culture trumps everything in business.

For a company to succeed, it is important to have good people, a good plan, and a good product or service. But far more important, or perhaps underlying and necessary for all of these things to exist, a company needs to have a defined culture.

What is a culture? It is a tight definition of what a company is, what it stands for, and what its values are. If there is a shared culture, with shared values, then every employee or team member will know what kind of behavior is expected of them. A defined culture need not have lots of rules that anticipate every possibility or "infraction" that might arise. This stifles creativity and collaboration. Culture is a living, breathing thing. It is everyone's responsibility to contribute to its maintenance and growth.

So, what is a great culture? It is one that puts ethics, team members, and service to the customer above all else. It is a culture without politics. It is a culture that is inclusive and diverse, a culture that values and provides opportunities for each team member, a culture that allows for failure and honors success. A culture like that will propel the people within a company to achieve all the success that they could possibly desire.

Reflection

53

**Choose your partners carefully, then rely
on them and nurture those relationships.**

I had the blessing of partnering with two extraordinary people in building my company. Part of the success of our relationship was that we complemented each other's skills, and we recognized that. Another part of our success was that we were willing to try to reach consensus on every decision. And, I suppose, part of our success was that everyone knew one of us had the majority vote.

Over time, we have expanded this partnership to include seven additional people. We have been very careful in selecting people whom we were confident would enhance and expand upon what the three of us had started.

But partnerships, like marriages, can be complicated. A partnership needs to be recognized and honored as an entity, as a living thing. It needs to be cultivated and nurtured over time. It needs to be valued and celebrated.

When one can put together the kinds of partnerships I have enjoyed throughout my career, one is very blessed.

VISION

Reflection

54

"Only he who keeps his eye fixed on the far horizon will find his right road."
Dag Hammarskjöld, the second Secretary General of the United Nations in the book, Markings

Markings, by Dag Hammarskjöld, is a great collection of wisdom that I read while attending Hobart College. In many respects, it was the inspiration for me to start writing down my own reflections many years ago.

Among the many things I learned from *Markings*, the above quotation is one of the most important. It is how I've tried to live my life. Perhaps it is only common sense that we must keep our eye on our future goals. Maybe that's why we ask little children what they want to be when they grow up.

Yet, unlike the answers those children may give—doctor, lawyer, teacher, nurse—the way I've interpreted this quote is not that we need to know specifically where we are going in life. Instead, we need to know what we want to have accomplished when we have completed our journey.

In this regard, I think it is better for a person to reflect: "I want to have accomplished something significant" or "I want to have improved the lives of my fellow man" or "I want to have had a meaningful family life" or "I want to have led a full and satisfying life" than it is to say, "I want to be president."

Focus on the horizon and let it inform your day-to-day decisions.

Reflection

55

"The mountain eagle is still higher than other birds upon the plain, even though they soar."

Ishmael, in the novel Moby Dick, *by Herman Melville*

Do not be satisfied simply getting things done or checking things off a list. Strive to be Melville's mountain eagle: be the best at everything you do, and you, too, will soar high. I cannot abide people who work by a checklist and then excuse poor performance, saying, "I'm only human." My response is that Beethoven, Michelangelo, Madame Curie, Harriet Tubman, Nelson Mandela... they, too, were only human.

"Good enough" never is. Always try to do better, no matter what it is you are doing. Never be done, finished, or satisfied. You have not equaled Michelangelo.

At The Bozzuto Group, one of our four corporate values is "Perfection, a goal worth pursuing." We all recognize that perfection is probably unachievable, but that doesn't mean that we shouldn't try to get there, in everything we do.

Excellence should never be optional! We do many things every day, often without focus, just to get them done. Whether it's the mundane, like shaving every morning, or the sublime, like kissing your spouse, put yourself into it and do it right. Stop making excuses for mediocrity. You can make excellence a habit—and you should. There is no reason to do anything in less than the best possible way.

VISION

We're not going to be perfect, but we're going to get damn close.

You will not always succeed, just as the eagle doesn't always get his prey. But you should never stop trying to soar.

Reflection
56

People work to be able to live, but they thrive at work when they have a reason to work that is bigger than they are.

People thrive in an organization with a vision that is bigger than making money, creating a product, or providing a service. Even when the goal is to make more money or to provide a better product or service, that doesn't get the juices flowing the way a larger vision does.

At The Bozzuto Group, we have developed, built, and managed many homes and apartments, yet our strong belief and vision has always been that the company's primary goal, our reason for existing, is to provide all our customers, regardless of income, with "sanctuary"—a place to live with the greatest of ease, with no inconvenience and no disruption. Far more than renting another apartment or building another home, this focus on a larger purpose is what motivates us. We come to work each day determined to create sanctuary for our customers—that is what brings us together and gives us purpose.

Reflection
57

> **To know where one has come from is
> not to be confined by that circumstance,
> but to be freed to be oneself.**

I know a fellow, a very successful man, who reminds me every time we talk that he grew up "on the other side of the tracks." The fact that he achieved great success despite his upbringing is indeed something to be proud of. But to carry that on your back like Sisyphus' rock is only to be weighed down and held back.

This doesn't mean that one should live a life of pretense. One shouldn't deny one's past any more than one should deny an illness. Yet knowing our roots doesn't mean being so defined by them that we are confined to a box. Nor should that knowledge limit our ability to define who we are or who we can become.

I am an Italian American, the product of a large family heavily steeped in our ethnic heritage and traditions. I am very proud of that. To this day, I bake my mother's pizza rustico, I grow tomatoes, peppers, and garlic in my garden, and I drink almost exclusively Italian wines. I smoke cigars, like my dad and granddad did, although fortunately of better quality. But I have not let my heritage interfere with my associations and friendships, control or limit my aspirations, or influence my business.

You see, your history is not the sole determinant of your future. But only you can ensure that.

RUNNING A COMPANY

Reflection

58

Create space between you and your competitors.
Focus on what makes you different, what your
customers value enough to pay you for, and then
build on it so you are absolutely the best.

At The Bozzuto Group, we have always attempted to create and operate what we think of as sanctuary—welcoming homes that are absolutely unexpected in the rental marketplace. Our customers love their apartments and are willing to pay a premium for them.

From the beginning, we determined that our apartment business would thrive and that we would become a market leader by providing service far beyond that which is normally offered in rental housing. We guaranteed 24-hour turn-around on maintenance calls, we allowed our renters flexible payment options, and we offered "out-of-town services," such as taking care of residents' pets when they were away. We recognized residents' birthdays with treats and today, continue introducing features that surprise and delight our customers.

More importantly, we hired staff for their heart rather than their skills. We hired this way on the belief that you can teach skills to a nice person a lot more easily than you can teach a skilled person to be nice.

Doing these things has allowed us to grow our company, building Bozzuto into a nationally recognized brand and adding significant value for our partners, our clients, and, most importantly, our residents.

Reflection
59

In business, surprise is always the enemy.

One of the worst offenses an employee can commit in an organization is to allow his or her supervisor to be surprised. It doesn't matter if the news is good news or bad news; no one wants to be surprised. A thoughtful team member will spend at least some of his or her time trying to anticipate what might go wrong and preparing for that in advance. Just as importantly, they will prepare their supervisors ahead of time if something looks like it might be going off track.

I think that often people who report directly to you want to spare you from having to deal with problems they anticipate, or they want to prove they can handle them on their own. One of the reasons I have always visited the properties we were responsible for was that I have found that people farther down in the organizational hierarchy and closer to the action are less inclined to hold back from sharing problems. Doing this helped me avoid many surprises, and in a few cases, even helped me to prevent problems from arising.

BOZZUTO AND ASSOCIATES

Working on four years old;
profitable, if barely.

Well-known, well-regarded,
a bright future;
if we survive.

Awesome.

TSB
11/1991

Reflection

60

"Only the paranoid survive!"

Andy Grove, founder and former CEO of INTEL

Every successful leader spends a portion of his time worrying about how a competitor can hurt him. It's not that your competitors are out to get you; it's that they are out to get you out of the way so they can succeed. Trust me, if you're not looking over your shoulder, analyzing your company and your competitors, trying to see your company's weakness and your competitors' strength, be assured that your competitors are doing so, and you won't be around very long.

Reflection

61

In business, cash really is king.

I will qualify the following by saying it is written from the perspective of someone who has taken a start-up to a 2,500-employee company, kept it private, and operated it with the intention of staying that way. I won't pretend that this rule applies to all types of businesses. But I do know that virtually every company needs credit to survive and grow.

Providers of credit, however, tend to be pretty cautious people who want to be sure that your business is going to be around for a while. Nothing gives them that assurance more than your having cash in the bank. In fact, to the consternation of my business partners, I have sometimes borrowed money rather than using the company's, just so that I can keep cash available. My theory has always been that I should borrow when I can, and save our cash, because there may come a time when I can't borrow, and then I will have that cash to draw from. Is this conservative? Yes. Do they teach it in business school? Probably not. Has it worked for me, and will it work for you? Absolutely.

Does this theory apply to individuals as well? I strongly believe so. My wife and I have always been regular savers and have thought living below our means was a prudent thing to do. My parents taught me that, and many of my friends reinforced it. You never know when something might come up—whether an opportunity or a need—and having had the discipline to save beforehand can be of immense value.

Reflection

62

Don't ever B.S. yourself

This seems obvious, but I've met many people in business who believe the world will be the way they want it to be, just because they want it to be that way. I've met people who are so good at selling that they actually believe the product or services are that good—even if they are not. Being analytical and intellectually honest is absolutely necessary for long-term success.

Reflection
63

The only guarantee when hiring is that you will be surprised.

Hiring someone to work with you is one of the most important decisions you will make. You should do so carefully and thoughtfully, interviewing extensively and checking references diligently. Then, pull the trigger and hope. Hope is all you can do at that point because you will be surprised. One hopes that your surprise will be on the upside. But, on occasion, that won't be the case. That's not an excuse for not doing the best job possible in selecting your candidate. It just means that you need to be assured you won't learn everything about the candidate until you've worked side by side with them for a while.

Reflection

64

Concentrate on, take advantage of, and build on your strengths. If you work hard to improve your weaknesses, all you will end up with is good weaknesses.

This may seem counter to much of what we are taught as children, but I believe it to be correct and wise. I have always had a terrible singing voice. If I had somehow gotten it into my head to become a vocalist, I may have ended up with a somewhat better sound, but I also would have starved to death.

I think it is important to figure out what we do that is uniquely better than anyone else, or at least better than most people, and then concentrate our energy on making that faculty or talent as good as we possibly can.

INITIATIVE AND RISK

RECIPE

The game of life:
One part happiness,
small touch of lemon.

TSB
10/30/1973

.

Reflection
65

Action creates opportunity.

It's better to be doing something rather than nothing at all. I have never really understood the concept of boredom, but I do know that boredom is a choice, not something with which you are afflicted, like a disease. I also know that the cure for boredom is action. Do something, anything, and you'll never be bored again. More importantly, you might find that you've done something productive that will lead you somewhere unexpected and wonderful.

Now, don't misunderstand this. I do believe in the importance of thoughtful reflection. I think there is great value and joy in just sitting and thinking. And, frankly, I consider this a form of action.

It is the sitting around, not doing or thinking of anything at all, that I believe is a waste of time—truly, a lost opportunity for growth.

Reflection

66

Fear is only of value when used as God intended: to propel initiative, action, and results.

Obviously, I have a bias for action. I sometimes think that if fear didn't exist, mankind would have had to invent it to propel us into improving our circumstances. Fear is a motivator. I truly believe that it is only through initiative and action that we can improve our environment, our quality of life, and even our chances for survival.

Think about how much the use of alternative energy has increased globally in the past two decades. Why has this happened? Because we have been shown by the scientific community that if we don't reduce our carbon emissions, global warming will change our planet into a largely unlivable environment. It is fear of that risk that has propelled the change. Fear is a good motivator.

On a more personal basis, consider why we work and why we strive for success. Certainly, after providing for our families, some of our motivation comes from our competitive nature and a desire to gratify our egos. But fundamentally, we push ourselves because we are afraid of the consequences of not doing so. In study after study of successful people, social scientists have shown that the majority of successful people work hard because, to a significant degree, they fear they will lose out to their peers. It is fear, not ambition or greed, that is often the motivator.

ADIEU

Goodbye to my youth
and to the opportunities missed.

I loved every minute
and now,
I am afraid of the future.

As I see fifty coming at me
with
wrinkles, pain and slowing of my faculties,
I see youth,
like a beautiful woman,
a laughing, carefree, loving woman
walking out of the tunnel of my past.

TSB
8/19/1996

Reflection

67

Take the initiative—otherwise, you'll spend all your time doing other people's bidding.

I remember in college reading the book *Sister Carrie* by Theodore Dreiser. In the book, a young country girl moves to the big city, where she has grand dreams but isn't able to achieve them, so she becomes a mistress to men who possess the wealth and station in life that she seeks. She perceives these men as superior to her, and she lives in their shadows.

My biggest take-away from this book is that this woman's entire character and whole life were defined for her by others. One of the most important life lessons I've learned is not to sit back and let others make decisions for you, nor define who you are as a person. All of us are responsible for our own lives; we define who we are by the decisions we make. We are the cumulative result of our decisions. We should not give our lives away—and that's exactly what we do when we let others define who we are or what we want to accomplish.

FINANCIAL DECISION-MAKING

Reflection

68

***Judge the gift second, the gift bearer first;
the opportunity second, the proposer first.***

In business, one gets many opportunities to pursue a certain course, to invest in a proposal, even to take a job. Far more important than the action itself is understanding the person or company with whom or which you will be working. I have never understood how people make decisions based only on price, or even just the attractiveness of what is being offered, without considering the source. Far more important is getting to know who you are buying from or with whom you will be working.

Reflection

69

The keys to investing are humility, skepticism, and optimism.

First, being humble about your investment strategy is to acknowledge you will never know as much as you should, nor as much as others do, about an investment opportunity.

Second, you have to understand that, despite all of their protestations to the contrary, no one else knows as much as they think they do, either. If they did, experts would never disagree.

Third, you should be optimistic that if you have humility and skepticism about investing, and you diversify whatever assets you have, over the long run you will probably make money.

Investing isn't a science with absolute assurance that one answer is the right one. Investing almost always involves human enterprise, chance, and risk. So don't ever believe that any one person, most especially you, has the answer.

THOUGHTS ON THE GREAT RECESSION

What keeps me going
is knowing
that the people I admire most
have thrived during much worse.

What keeps me going
is knowing
that my seeming self-confidence, poise and balance,
and the emphasis is on the word "seeming,"
is what keeps those who work with me
confident.

And, ironically, it feeds on itself.
The bankers, the lenders
trust us
because we seem to know what we're doing.

God, if they only knew how nervous
I sometimes am,
they'd take their money and run.

What keeps me going
is knowing that I have a strong desire
to deliver a successful company
into the hands of the next generation.

What keeps me going
is that I know there are opportunities
in this mess.

What keeps me going
is that, most often,
it's fun.

TSB
1/2009

Reflection

70

**The financial world is divided into
two groups—optimists and pessimists.
Each is right about half the time.**

We all know Pollyannas, people who think everything will always work out. And, given enough time, they are often right. But there are also those who are convinced everything is likely to fail. There is merit to that position as well, at least on occasion. Most of us fall into one group or the other.

There is no doubt that I am an optimist. Nonetheless, when making investment decisions, I believe we should try to control our natural instinct toward optimism or pessimism, and put some of our money on the other side of the equation.

Always ask the question, "What if…?"

Reflection
71

"*Don't underestimate the need to save money.*"

Most of us struggle to live by this maxim, which was one that my Great Depression-era dad drilled into me. But it's worth keeping in mind.

My father was a workingman who never earned more than $7,500 a year working in a factory. A compulsive saver, he was able to buy a home, an oil business, and a second piece of property—and send three kids to college. He died leaving a small estate and no debt.

My dad taught my family that we should live within our means, and that if we couldn't pay cash for something, we probably didn't need to own it. While this is pretty old-fashioned and probably totally unrealistic today, the idea of saving some money and building a savings fund will never go out of date.

SUCCESS AND FAILURE

Reflection

72

War is won before the battle takes place.

This simply means: prepare, prepare, prepare. I was never the brightest, nor the most intuitive, nor the most creative person in my class in school. During my career, however, I did work as hard and prepared as much as anyone I've ever met. And it always seemed that the more thoroughly and carefully I prepared, the better I did. Similarly, I think if one studies battles or business success, the victory often goes to the warrior who is best prepared.

Reflection

73

**Contests, games, wars, and negotiations
are most often won by the person who
retains her confidence the longest.**

I suspect everyone will acknowledge the importance of self-confidence. How often do we watch two equally qualified people and see that the one who succeeds is the person who has the self-esteem to stand up and be noticed and the inner strength to know they can survive failure? There can be no doubt that the person who is most confident—not arrogant—is usually the one who thrives. The challenge is maintaining that confidence in the face of adversity. He who does that—whether a general at war or a businessperson in a negotiation—is the one who will usually come out ahead.

How we maintain that self-confidence is probably as varied as there are people who might read this. For me, it has been by focusing on the strength of my position and not on my weakness vis-à-vis my opponent. I am always surprised in business by how often I hear people on one team talking about their team's weaknesses and the strengths of their adversary. Now, please don't misunderstand this. I have always believed it critical to understand and thoroughly evaluate my competitor's strengths and fully understand my weaknesses, but only so that I know how to overcome them. I think it is by understanding my strengths and how to use them that I am able to maintain confidence and achieve some degree of success.

Reflection

74

Focus on the doing and the reward will be success.

Sometimes people who are dissatisfied with their current position and anxious to advance get frustrated and just "phone it in." That is, they perform in a way that shows they are not thrilled with what they are doing. Perhaps unintentionally, they are broadcasting that they are not to be depended upon.

To be successful, one should focus on the job at hand and be better at it than anyone could possibly expect. Results count, and people will notice! So, if you really want to advance in your career, do the job you're assigned—and produce results! Then, when you chase the next opportunity, it will be yours for the asking.

A PRAYER

Give me strength not to be satisfied with small success

and

the wisdom to be grateful for each of them.

TSB

Reflection
75

Frequently the hangover that follows a great victory is an even greater depression.

Every one of us who has ever pursued a great challenge and won is aware that a sense of dissatisfaction, disappointment, or dismay often follows the victory celebration. This occurs for any number of reasons, better explained by a psychologist than by me, but shouldn't ever be a surprise.

Reflection

76

Look at the quality of the decision-making process, not just the outcome.

It is incumbent on all of us, especially those of us running an en-terprise, not only to be aware of the outcome of our efforts, but also to try to understand what caused that outcome. So often I have found that we are ready to move on to the next thing we are doing and accept the results of what we have done before, often without trying to learn from what we've done. If we try to do something and it is not as successful as we thought it was going to be, we have to try to learn why so we have a better shot at getting it right the next time. The same thing is true if we've had a great success. We should stop and ask why.

Reflection

77

**The glow of a successful achievement,
uncelebrated at the time,
will always be tarnished by delay.**

This is as important in one's personal life as it is in running a business. Life is a struggle, and when we achieve a goal, we should never hesitate to celebrate it. If we delay doing so, the joy will be diminished by the effort involved in the next undertaking.

At Bozzuto, we have a wall-mounted bell, given to me years ago by my parents, around which we frequently gather to let someone who's had an achievement ring in their success. Whether you buy a bell or give a pat on the back, don't forget to celebrate and congratulate.

Reflection

78

When the item being sold is in high demand, the successful purchaser is often the best salesman.

When you think about the buy-and-sell transaction, particularly when you are contemplating a large transaction, it is common to think that the seller will always select the buyer who is willing to pay the highest price. If this were true, there would be no hope for the small competitor and the individual just getting started. Everything would be about dollars and nothing else. But frequently, it has been my experience that a seller looks for other things beyond, or perhaps in addition to, the best price she or he can get. The seller is always looking for certainty of execution. Beyond that, the seller is often looking for the fewest hassles in effectuation of the sale. Sometimes, particularly when the seller feels some sentimental attachment to the object being sold, the seller is looking to the character of the buyer.

For all of these reasons, I have long maintained that in a competition, the best purchaser is often the best salesman—that is, the one most capable and with the greatest facility of convincing the seller that the price is reasonable, the closing will in fact take place as scheduled, that it will be reasonably painless, and that the item being sold will be well taken care of in the future.

CREATIVITY AND INNOVATION

EFFERVESCENCE

Joy, sorrow, love, sadness,
romance, glee, pain, beauty,
passion—
only a smattering of the numerous stops on the
transit line of life.

I love life:
its Pepsi-Cola action,
its love-story peace,
its meaningfulness, and
its absurdity.
Its pressures and excitement,
its monotony and routine.

I feel like a
Cracker Jack waiting for someone
to open my box
so that I can pop out.

TSB
3/19/1973

Reflection

79

Money is easy to find.
It's ideas that are in short supply.

In our capitalistic world, I have found that two of the variables most critical to success are money and ideas. What I have also found is that money is far more readily available than are new and useful ideas. This is not to say that capital is ever easy to get or that there aren't a fair number of opportunities passed along on a regular basis; it's just that well-thought-out ideas, creative suggestions, and really good opportunities are all too rare. Fresh ideas are invaluable to success.

Reflection

80

Those who thrive will be those who figure out new ways to do things and new things to do.

I thought about this as I prepared for a speech I was to present to the Washington, D.C. chapter of the Urban Land Institute when they recognized me with a Lifetime Achievement Award in the fall of 2008. Although receiving the award was a high honor and one of which I was quite proud, the idea of having to give an uplifting speech to 500 people in the real estate business in the midst of the worst recession any of us had ever seen, was a little intimidating.

As I prepared for my speech, it occurred to me that while we were learning on a daily basis of collapsing businesses and a faltering economy, we were routinely hearing pundits assert that "this time is different." By this, they were suggesting that what the economy was going through was not your garden-variety recession, but something truly revolutionary and monumental, something that would change our entire economic system and our way of life. This struck me at the time, and still does, as overwrought, even ludicrous.

After all, every moment in time is unique, every event different, every historical instance distinctive. Today will always be different from yesterday and tomorrow. Yet at the same time, there are patterns in history and a continuity to events, just as there are constants that have governed success throughout time. What seemed most important to me then, particularly at that time of economic flux, was the need to try something new, or to figure out a way to do something old in a better way.

I have long believed that recessions are probably healthful for the economy in that they foster an environment of creativity and a time when people are willing and pressed to try new things. However, we needn't wait for a recession to be creative.

Reflection

81

When you have a problem, try everything...
success usually comes to those who experiment.
I call this "management by fiddling around."

I have always been intrigued by the idea held by some that there is a single solution to every problem. Maybe there is, but in my experience, one can get into far deeper trouble wasting time trying to find that perfect solution. My belief is that when something is wrong, you generally can't afford to test alternative remedies one by one. You have to try a number of things simultaneously. At worst, you will have eliminated a lot of possible solutions.

Reflection

82

Dig the hole in another place.

I learned this lesson from my wise colleague, Ray Blank. When we had a dilemma at work, a situation where we were being forced to choose between two seemingly unattractive alternatives, Ray would often suggest that "we dig the hole in a different place." He meant that sometimes, maybe even frequently, we constrain ourselves to two choices when there are actually other ways of solving or even avoiding the problem we are dealing with. This requires almost a retraining of our minds because all too often, perhaps ever since childhood, we have been making choices we don't have to make. Find that unexplored option.

Reflection

83

Creativity without discipline is chaos!

I love creative people, but for creativity to result in accomplishment, one needs discipline. Throughout history, the creative people who have most impacted human life have been those who knew how to discipline their creativity—either on their own, or by working with someone who balanced their creativity with a practical, productive approach.

Think, for example, of Thomas Edison, perhaps America's most prolific inventor. Developing a commercially viable electric light bulb was extraordinary and would have made him famous, even if he had done nothing else. Having the discipline to follow that with a patent for electricity distribution and then to create a company to distribute electricity is what made him very successful.

Reflection

84

Keep your options open as long as possible.

Early in my career, I learned this rule from a colleague. When I first saw this in action, I was as frustrated by it as many of my family and colleagues have been since I've adopted it. By this statement, I mean that you shouldn't just jump to a solution the minute you confront a problem. You should evaluate it, consider it from all dimensions, look at alternatives, and prolong your decision as long as practical to be as certain as you can. But do make a decision!

Reflection

85

**"It is not the strongest of the species that
survive, nor the most intelligent, but the
most responsive to change."**

Anonymous

The ability to adjust to changes in one's environment is generally
accepted as a key determinant of long-term Darwinian survival.
(The dinosaurs were the strongest species on Earth at the time of
their eclipse, and see where that got them.)

It is equally true that success in business is frequently tied to an
ability and willingness to adapt to different situations and changing
circumstances.

I learned this lesson in spades when I worked for a company that
built its entire, very profitable operating model around a type of
financing that was completely dependent on a single provision in
the federal tax code. In 1986, when that provision was eliminated,
the company had nowhere to go and ultimately went out of
business. It wasn't that the change in the tax law was a surprise.
Everyone knew this was a possibility, and spent lots of time and
money trying to fight it. We did everything, in fact, except what was
most important. We did not prepare a business model that would
work without that favorable tax provision.

In addition to one's ability to make wise decisions while on the
job, an ability to work with different types of people in different

situations, and to be comfortable in different environments, will help in advancing a career. But even beyond that, being able to find a sense of ease in social and professional settings will just make life more pleasurable.

One of the joys of my life has been that I get to spend time with a wide variety of people from an extraordinarily diverse collection of backgrounds: from my construction colleagues at Bozzuto to the college professors at Hobart & William Smith Colleges, where I serve on the board; from bank presidents and wealthy investors to customers in our affordable housing communities. I suspect that my ability to not only get along with people in all of these groups, but also to enjoy them, has contributed to whatever success I've achieved.

So, learn to adjust. Teach your children to do so. The world is not designed around our comfort, or theirs. There is no reward for defining yourself by what or who annoys you. Learn to enjoy where you find yourself, learn to adapt, learn to anticipate and accommodate change. You will not only survive, you will thrive.

THANKSGIVING

We thank you, Lord
for our health, that
makes life easy;

for our challenges, that
make life interesting;

for our wealth, that
makes life comfortable;

for our country, that
makes life free;

for our friends, that
make life enjoyable;

for our family, that
makes life complete;

and
for our love, that
makes life worth living.

TSB
1991

ACKNOWLEDGEMENTS

Acknowledgements

Let me begin by thanking my wife, Barbara. She has supported me and encouraged me to write this book, as she has done with everything else I've attempted in my life. It was she who gave me the blank journals throughout the years into which I scribbled these reflections. It was she with whom I/we have turned the blank journal that was our life fifty years ago into something of which we could be proud.

My family has been a constant source of love and inspiration, especially my daughter, Lexie, my son and successor as the CEO of Bozzuto, Toby, and my beautiful grandchildren, Sofia, Allie, Annie, Jay, Thomas, and Charlie.

This book would not be in your hands right now if not for Julie Smith, my colleague of thirty years, whose idea it was to publish these reflections and make them available to our business associates, clients, partners, and friends. I thank her for the push to do that, and for reading early drafts and making this a stronger book.

My business partners and co-founders in creating The Bozzuto Group, Rick Mostyn and John Slidell, have been essential companions in determining what our company would become. Whatever we've done, we've done together. This book is a tribute to that partnership.

Roger Hare, my college roommate and close friend of more than fifty years, not only gave me great feedback on early drafts of this book, but when a house fire destroyed my copy of Dag Hammarskjöld's *Markings*, the book that originally inspired me to write down my thoughts, Roger gave me his.

I'd like to thank my editor, Adrienne Hand, who helped translate what was originally written for my personal consumption into something a lot more polished and understandable. Thank you, Adrienne, for helping me to really think through and define, and even eliminate, a few of these reflections.

I would also like to thank Sarah Smith for her beautiful illustrations. Chintimini Keith, Samantha Schlemm, and Rebecca Breslin on the design team created a book that is both beautiful and true to the original idea of a journal. Jamie Gorski provided wise guidance, and Matthew McGrath and his team at PCA Printing produced a lovely book.

Finally, I would like to thank my colleagues at The Bozzuto Group. Each of you has helped me convert a dream into a reality. You have helped John, Rick, Toby, Julie, the other partners, and me make Bozzuto into a world-class real estate company and service provider. As I say over and over, it is my life's greatest honor to be able to work alongside all of you. Thank you.

Tom